SALVATIONS

LIFE UNDER DARKNESS

LOUISE JURY DEAN

This book is dedicated to all those

who have held me

without hurting me

Contents

Contents

Foreword

Louise and I have been friends since our first grades and I feel immensely proud writing a foreword for her book. We have always bonded over our nerdy interests. In this collection of poems written by my dear friend, she aims to scrupulously highlight the importance of peace and salvation. Something that can be obtained by anyone and everyone.

Poems about destruction, love and friendship, I reckon go hand in hand. To each poem, Dean brings immense understanding of humanity. This collection may not be dazzled with fancy and exuberant words but the simple language targets all audiences to read and gain from the collection.

Salvation is possible for everyone. The harder you chase it, the more difficult it is to attain.

-Siddhi Gupta

Preface

Hello, this is the author here.

salvations, to be honest, was never meant to happen. I was writing another novel but lost motivation so I stopped. Then one day I wrote a poem called 'crawler', I didn't find it good enough so I gave up poetry too.

But then one blessed night I wrote another poem, then another and then another. I wrote nine poems that night. I started writing poems everyday. Slowly I started appreciating my work and the motivation came back. I wrote at speeds both blazing and infuriating.

I started editing my book and looking for publishers to get work started. I wanted something free. As a fifteen year old I had zero money and a million mental problems.

Whatever I could do, I have done. I worte this book quite secretly. No one but me knew about it. This book is my salvation. It has saved me from betraying my own self.

If you find this book by any means relatable, I send you my love.

LJD

saturyday, 11 june

Acknowledgements

This book has taken pain, a lot of it.

and ofcourse I haven't done it without help

But I would love to thank the following people:

Notion press for creating a platform to help so many young publishers like me to publish their dream book.

Suzy Hazels form pexels for a lot of her beautiful vintage found photos.

and my dear friend siddhi (who is great at criticizing books) for write the foreword. (someone had to write it lol)

Prologue

A beauty that resents freedom

    Crumbles

    and rises

    a new bird

    flying on wings

    of love

    and destruction

1. Crawler

When little insects crawl on my legs
I dont push them away
I just let them crawl
Reminds me of when you would
crawl all over my body
Only that you weren't an insect,
You were a lizard
A big Salamander
I remember how you would crawl with your blazing feet
You'd dance
That'd peel the skin off my thighs
You did it until all my muscles were exposed
Until I was a bloody mess
Then I finally breathed
and you were blown away.

take my bare dead body to church

2. In pursuit of the White Dragon

I am hallucinated by life
It's all that I feel
It's all that I fear
Ah isn't it so very dramatic?
The way things seem to do themselves
I see an electric White Dragon in the distance
While I sit in the mouth
of a Dying Phoenix
Try as I might
The Phoenix won't move his Jaw
but I can see from a small whole I chewed out on his lip
He feeds on my Undying Fire
I keep him alive as I burn
If only I had enough—
courage to kill myself
I'd be free
but then there is my soul
A wanderer's soul
It won't let me die
until I have circumnavigated the world

SALVATIONS

I keep on
with the radio on
I see beauty inside the Phoenix's body
Yet still inside, I feel alone
I am allied with my soul
but
now
I
have found a way
I will give my fire away to my soul for safekeeping
and the Phoenix will think I am dead
he will quickly open his jaw
in fear of dying
searching for a new life support
and
I
will run out as quick as possible
take my fire back from my soul
et voila the phoenix is tricked
now here I am
damned
but free as fuck
running to my dear
darling white dragon.

let the roses rest in your throat

SALVATIONS

3. E

But I never knew
what soft hands felt like
or what pure happy is
who really cares tho?
now that I've seen Saturn dance
I've seen it engaged to the sun
and I have tried to become you
even when I know I can't
You are too surreal
and it infuriates me how you can still manage to be real
you are beautiful
you are kind
you are fucking blind
You give like an angel
You never need or want
I've slept for the both of us
I've hated for the both of us
You eccentric woman
I am you
You are me
but we are still five hundred twenty million light-years apart
Why do you hate me so much

SALVATIONS

I couldn't aspire
for anything higher
Your destruction day is the same day
as the day of my salvation
I can't speak
I can't write
all because of you
and I've never been on long motorcycle rides
Unlike you
You are such a fucking rose
Beautiful
Taste like Gold
Smell like heaven
But honey you'd be too good to be real
So you've got thorns
You've stabbed and pricked my flesh
You've been down my throat
but I vomited you right back
I can never digest you
You are too evil.

beauty is relative on Earth, outside it? not so much

4. Clopes

I close my eyes

The fumes go wilder

I see no Sun down here

in this little chamber

but I am heated up

My body grows stiffer and softer each day

I am crying downtown

In this narrow chamber

I have layed my residence

It's filled with smoke

Black and Blue

it dances in my lungs

balloons up and creates a void

In which swims my fragile soul

It's all I can see

I can't breathe

I can't swim

I can't be

so I perfume myself with you

Wish I was her

Wish I am me

but even after all the deprived children, men and women in me

the sun never sets on us
my darling fantasy
I can't stop
I keep going on and on
I have been caught
in acts of romance with you
several times
but my hands still grab you
and we go down to our hidden chamber
for tying ourselves
in a fearful, enchanting, terrific romance
and when we are done
I hide you and your wife
somewhere safe
but not unexplored
only to be discovered again
and I shower your sweet essence off of my body
I hate to do it
but I have to do it
or they might catch us
at this point tho
it doesn't even matter
they can never separate us
We were made for each other

happy birthday dear reader

5. The Other Girl

I walk around
Men of the future
behind my ass
Women staring at me
Women of culture
of manner
of shame
of honor
Staring down at me hard
I laugh
I scream
I enjoy
with my kind of people
they engirth me
I engirth them
much to the man's disappointment
anger
jealousy
some shy and far
some hateful but near
and some sweet and close
I have my eyes over them

Me,

their momma

All women who bore my babies in their belly

even the one who bore me

Shoot strong glances of fire like detestation

I open my mouth wide

to swallow them

My stomach digests them well

I smile as the acid in me boils

But I stay quiet

Me, the other girl

and then the ocean sneezed a magnificent sneeze

6. Kanpur

A city

A self-destructive city

with men of freedom

wild in the eye

stripping down to their skeletons

and in the filthy summers

I see how their eyes go blind

yet they move

with madness, toil, dust, and lust

I feel them grow into black blazing ghosts

I watch as they move their rotten limbs

A torso churned out of size

Minds

Diving deep and hollow

Mimicking a fake health

I see women rolled up in linen

of a quality that sucks

bags and bags and bags of dicks

Their slant, pleasing bodies

moving downward

They use a tiny length of the road

only to save

Their eyes
wide but narrowed
their brightness, stolen away
forever
pour toujours
Sultry was the summer the day
She was dragged away
Fear, Hate, Pain, and a crate of food
that is thrown away
licked by creatures of all sizes
great and small
of all colors
grey and blonde
Scared of what these women realize are animals
They create a universe
of self-hate, self envy, and maybe self-love
They aren't happy
They have after all
Nobody
to teach
why the atmosphere is so dreary
with every last human being
rolling flesh of their bodies
peeling it out
some to prove their worth
some to feed their baby
and some like me

just to feel
and then descends the rush of the night
The rush I feel
The rush I love
She finally commences to breathe
The reality of this city
The mother, The giver
The savior and the une of this city
a WHORE
She is the essence
She is the soul
She is the life support of this city
She comes out

cums out

when it is minuit
She is fucked by
hundreds
thousands
millions
every eery second
She is fortunate cause
They fuck her to a rhythm
She cries like an angel
she gasps
She sighs oh so well
Her mere glance could light up the sky
better than Diwali

LOUISE JURY DEAN

A woman so powerful
could melt me in a moment
fortunate I've never met her
She's given birth to a billion children
Children with runaway fathers
and a mother who drinks
She's slutty, She brightens the room
every time she enters
She's the prettiest in every photo
Photo season never runs out for her
She's ruined the best minds of her generation
by drugs
by drinks
by smokes
She runs on every road
and tells everyone
stories of pleasure
of loss
of gain
of slather of pain
hurt and stains
She enchants every boy
and a few girls like me
and then she takes them
like the pide piper of Hamelin
She lures them into the ocean of murder, hate, crime
and The Grand Holy Disease

She is Kanpur
My mother city.

Will Maddie Klein ever be fucked to a rythm again

7. Noir

As a fool
I tread where angels fear to
I am attracted to places
where darkness plunders
even god himself
Satan's been following me
for quite a long time now
A wealthy devil
My deceitful baby
resisting happy
joy
pretty
welcoming all fear
pleasure
magnificence
Roaming in pits of hell
with everyone's eyes
lower than the last circle
The sound of darkness
of dishonor
The scream of Sin
The hatred that

beauty resents
The love that I care for
all BURNS.

the road to heaven commences at the bottom of your heart

8. To the Moon

Every night I fly to the moon
with leather boots
a leather jacket
and a short white dress
that exposes my thighs
I go high
I go high
I am high
My long and pretty hair
welcomes winds from both directions
They sway hard and bad
They are black, shiny and they gleam
like my smile
every night I transform
myself into an angel
and I create Tornadoes
and Tsunamis
and Hurricanes
first I destroy earth
Then I light a smoke
and open a beer
sit on the moon

and now
I destroy Myself.

I'd love to call, but my phone is out of reach

9. Momma

She raged

I raged back

but my rage was more defensive

not attack

I couldn't do shit

I couldn't control my mind

that's wild as fuck

So she hit me

While I was on temperature

I swallowed the pain

I swallowed my own rain

She regretted while she did it

but she

She didn't stop

kept going on

attacked till I was bruised

Black and Blue

Tears like a mermaid's pearls

in my eyes

Happiness just walking by

and I

I cry

and yell back
I do it till she
gives up in fear
and in the end
we both Die.

there's sweetness and joy in every little sadness

10. We in Love

It's hard to confess
that I love you
and it's easy to
let you in
but hard to keep you out
I still keep you out
My heart turns
into a camera
made of stone
That records everything sad and bad
Oh my little cat
Maybe it's hard to be good to me
as a hundred people make me feel
but you hold out your arms
you try to keep me safe
but to try to keep a destructive goddess safe
is like citrus in your eyes
It will hurt you
and you will grow tired
I hurt you
You hurt me
We hurt us

and that's how we make love
Everything I've told you
Everything I've told me
It doesn't matter now
Cause you are already in.

she was followed to hell, her friend was just so loyal

11. Hélène

Your golden curls hang
all the way down to your ass
your white and red and blue
dresses twirl violent in motion
You move like an angel
Sweet baby, give him a kiss
Let him fuck you longer
Dance with him all around the room
Like a purple ballerine
Let the clouds come
down to raise you up
Let the tarot reader fix
your eccentric wedding
You shine like diamonds
You are loved by all
Everybody's girl
Sad heroine to no hero
A blue water snake in disguise
You dance the whole town
on your slender fingers
Like sweetness dissolved in lime
Your gravity yells

and people attract
They treat you like shit
The men you've had
The boys you've ruined
Rushing all the time
like a rat in New York
Settle down a little
Sleep.

blue skies and apple pies

12. Street's Boy

Your silence is like
friction to my mind
I cry for you to speak
You resist
all of me
We're crazy in love
Yet worlds apart
Let's go on a spree
Let's unfold universes
Let's yell on the streets
Graffiti and peach
Leather
Sweet Weather
and Life
finally coming around
Forgive my failure
to stay earlier
We're together
you roam around
you've got a mind made of gold
ruined by addiction
Diamonds in your eyes

and again
friction to my mind
We see everything
You've got Guns
You've got Roses
and I love
your filthy photo poses
You ride with me
on all of your horses
We laugh with
all of your friends
We drink
We drag
We have fun
We fucking live.

you are what you are

13. Who Else Longs For Paradise?

I am so far from Paradise
It's not yet here
I see God every day
but in a Coffin
Will it take another eternity?
Oh! what is this?
I am so goddamned impatient
Come to me Oh Paradise
let me live
let me breathe
my mind
Torn
my heart
Barred
my wings
Clipped
my legs
Chopped
and my hands?
Tied!

SALVATIONS

I'll yell
I'll scream
It won't matter
The holy disease will
still eat me
What I'm afraid of is
that I'll be black pulp
before I reach
Paradise.

paradise is slowly shattering

14. Holy water

I'll rise up to the sky
I've been down too long
I've been in too long
Then I'll swim in Monna's Oceans
and I'll fill them up
the way I filled up
Hepburn's moon river
I'll quench hell's thirst
and honey
if you ask nicely
I'll fill up your silent little pond
So when you wake up tomorrow
you'll have a place to drown in
and then you'll thank me
You'll say
"Thank you baby
Thank you for your Golden tears"
"Now I can finally feel
finally have the water
running between my thighs"
"and I can finally die"

when she danced the room caught fire

15. Vicente Silva

Black beauty
diamond mind
poems on the same theme
every time
holds my hand
till the end of the road
I keep my destruction
but he talks
and delays the hour
He drinks from a different spring
He can actually control his limbs
He's taught me so much
How to move mountains
and differentiate winds
He observes like a dancer
twirling in space and time
To see his torso
I have to look up
a 1000 feet high
He's so God
He is so pretty
Sometimes he's nervous and shitty

Forgives like an angel
and asks for forgiveness
even for me
He is my little friend
His upper stories
are sound
brave
proud
Only 15
but walks the streets and gleams
glitters like saturn's rings
He knows what he does
He learns what he sees
Born to people
with the art of raising and appreciation
an Intuition of Creation
Vicente, my best friend.

i will love you till the end of all space and time

16. Younger Words

If you were taught shame
before you were taught
how to love your body
welcome to my world
you are just like me

Chapter17

Sweet baby Jane
Full of treason
My mind can take no more
and you are the reason

Chapter18

Hold me tighter
tonight
else I might lose my mind
and run away

Chapter19

Villany is freedom

Heroism is destruction

Chapter 20

Plan
Your last trip tonight
Take
The last boat
because
You are in the jungle baby
You are gonna die

Chapter21

Let the Sun rain down
Hydrogen and Helium
on me
I need to feel fucking something

Chapter 22

I have a loving mother
father
family
but I am unhappy
If love is not enough
what is?

Chapter 23

Shake every bit
of your body tonight
Dance like
no one's watching
Live like
no one's listening

Chapter 24

Sometimes I feel
like I am not even here
Time moves slow for me
Slower than the entire rest of the world

Chapter25

My life
will ebb
My life
will flow
with

or

without you

Chapter26

Dear Pluto
I feel for you
I understand
what its like
to be pushed away.

Chapter27

Last night
I dreamt
of you being the Charismatic Young Cult Leader
I always wanted
You held me in your arms
Put the gun on my stomach
and
BANG BANG
you shot me down

Chapter28

Lingering outside the bar
in hopes of finding
that guy
Who would buy me a drink
the one that I like

Chapter 29

The black night descends
I saw your gleaming eyes
and grin
like a madman's
and I knew
just what you were
about to do

Chapter30

Everything you hide
All the secrets that you keep
in deep
will one day come out
you might feel
devastated

or

profane
but that sould be alright

Chapter 31

Last girl on the planet
Last bottle of wine
Last bit of metal
Let it begin

Chapter32

A 70-year-old saint
with the profanity
of a lost sailor
who treats
water like it's sand.

LOUISE JURY DEAN